CALLING ALL YOUTH

Phoenix De Vries

BALBOA
PRESS

A DIVISION OF HAY HOUSE

Balboa Press books may be ordered through booksellers or by contacting:

Balboa Press
A Division of Hay House
1663 Liberty Drive
Bloomington, IN 47403
www.balboapress.com.au
1 (877) 407-4847

Print information available on the last page.

ISBN: 978-1-5043-0377-4 (sc)
ISBN: 978-1-5043-0378-1 (e)

Balboa Press rev. date: 08/29/2016

Welcome
to the
twenty-first century.

Welcome
to
planet
Earth,
to
the time of
mankind and technology.

The universe is vast and filled with endless possibilities.

Your mission, your destiny—should you choose to
accept it—is to find
and to know your authentic soul.

Your mission—should you choose it—is to stay alive, not to
die fast, but to live the fullest life you can. Become alive to
life. Recognise your spirituality.

Give yourself permission to manifest your glorious soul
in order to live the life you chose before coming here to
Mother Earth.

Your destiny is now, and you must choose:

- light over dark
- love over hate
- enlightenment over ignorance
- awareness and learning
- being
- respect
- harmony within chaos
- remembrance than forgetting
- play and humour
- observation

Masters of the universe, know that you are spiritual beings having a physical experience on earth. You are not a robot, but you are living in a robotic age, where you will see robots come of age.

In the twenty-first century, humanity has entered into a relationship in which an individual's personal life intimately interacts with technology. We soon will plunge our lives completely into the digital world, consuming all that has made us human.

Let's not allow the world to be destroyed by ignorance. Let's not allow the world to be run by robots or artificial intelligence but by natural loving, that we as humans are capable of doing.

You are unique; your soul comes first from the Divine, the physical form, from the seed of man, and born from the womb of a woman.

We Are Born with This Connection

No future robot can create this amazing, natural, intelligent feat. We are a reflection of the divine God and Goddess. Your soul is made from Spirit, and that soul is connected to all living things in the universe.

You belong to the Divine Creator who is divine intelligence. Masters of the universe, that awareness is a power that lives in your heart, and what's more, it's in everything and everywhere. When you look closer into all living things, you see beauty in everything. Connect with this divine intelligence.

One of the biggest tests that the Navy SEALs use to train their cadets is an exercise for overcoming fear, in which the recruits are not allowed to breathe under water. Why is it that these trainees are challenged in this way? Because fear stops our potential.

Let's not take for granted the air, which is provided for us freely by Mother Earth. Connect to air and breathe. Breathe, my friend, breathe in that beautiful air; slowly fill your lungs with good, clean air every day.

You Need Connection, Like You Need the Air to Breathe

You are a living being, connected to this universe. Know that you belong to and are interconnected with this loving oneness.

Within This Oneness Is an Ocean of Loving Kindness

To be masters of the universe, find a connection each day; whether you find this connection in yourself, your work, your home, your relationships, do it.

We need connection to our brothers and sisters of like mind, soul, and heart. We need connection to the earth and sky as mother and father.

Connect

Let yourself experience connection. You may choose to connect every day with something natural on this wondrous planet called Earth. Choose to connect with a loving friend, be it an animal, nature, or a person. We are all interconnected by the grace of God or Goddess, Divine Mother or Divine Father.

Before you rise in the morning, be quiet and still for one minute, in what is known as the alpha state, and tune into this loving inner being that resides within you—your inner self! Give thanks for the new day, ask for protection, ask for loving guidance, and then set your intention. Make this your ritual each day.

State, "May the experience of the day, for my growth and development, be the best, and with your loving support, I shall be all that I can be and more."

Dare to Be

Then Let Go

Trust

Your higher self wants the best for you. When you realise this, it will create harmony within and bring a feeling of tranquility and peace.

Who are we? Are we powerful creators who have forgotten our mastery? It's true that we are made from light particles, from quantum energy. And you are not alone. You have an internal partner.

The Best Partner for You is Your Inner Self

Get up and live your day in confidence, come what may. Let the day begin by trusting the your inner light. Allow your inner self to have a voice, and listen quietly to what it has to say. Eventually you will recognise the small still voice within.

At the end of each day, before you go to sleep, reflect on how your day went, ask yourself, *What have I learnt today? What did I love and appreciate about myself this day? and ….. remember;* Sleep is fundamental for revitalisation of mind and body.

Eureka! It Works

Many thinkers throughout history have used this technique of asking, before going to sleep at night, for answers to problems they had grappled with during their days.

Let your inner self work for you, and you shall have profound results. Your answers may come through dreams or come to you intuitively upon waking. They may come through an inspirational idea.

Trust in Your Intuition

Know that you are created in love, that is, divine love. This is not human love, but divine love, unconditional love. Discover this love within your very own inner self. It is the force that binds all as one.

We are powerful creators. We live in a world that exists independently, yet we are so intimately connected, and we are participators—co creators—within this universe that is so amazingly our home.

You are created from the divine spark of the universe.

From Light

Light comes not from darkness, because darkness is the absence of light. (Ancient, Mystical Order, Rosae Crucis)

This universe is divine intelligence, and this divine intelligence permeates throughout the universe, similar to a hologram within a hologram; it is endless. Within your very cells, this intelligence is continuously creating balance between the positive and negative for the good of the whole.

Today, scientists talk about quantum particles, how they are always connected to one another and how they communicate, in both the past and the future. Yet at the same time, these particles can change.

Change is happening all the time. Just as relationships have a way of shifting, of changing, of moving and flowing, transformation is a natural progression. We have the ability to transform our lives in order to become better each day.

Transformation occurs within the very cells of our body, even in the tiny protons. Even scientists in the modern world have proven that photons (a fundamental particle of visible light) can change the past into the present, even though the past has already happened.

Letting go of the past instantly allows us to live in the present, in the now. In other words, masters of the universe, with this knowledge, we can change the beliefs that hold us back and truly reach for the stars in order to reach our full potential through the force of our own consciousness. Your mastery, should you choose to take this mission, is to become aware of your consciousness. Infinite consciousness permeates throughout the universe.

"All matter originates and exists only by virtue of a force which brings the particle of an atom to vibration and holds this most minute solar system of the atom together. We must assume behind this force the existence of a conscious and intelligent mind. This mind is the matrix of all matter."
— Max Planck

You may understand this universal soul more clearly in the context of the movie, *The Matrix*, the matrix of all matter and non-matter.

The Interconnected Web of Life

Within this scope, quantum possibilities are endless. Divine love is yours, to have and to hold forever. Photons are telling us that, simply by imagining peace and abundance within our minds and hearts, instantly, it becomes a field of light that emanates outward to interact with all living things.

Be Curious

Align with the feelings of your hearts, of your emotions and your thoughts, knowing that you are in oneness with your Divine Father and Divine Mother.

These feelings and emotions of higher love and inner connections are your inheritance. Embrace them, as they belong you. Don't allow anyone, or anything, to take these things away from you.

How simple is it? It's not that easy. Let's break it down.

There are two basic emotions that we as humans can choose from: Love or fear. The ancient mystics talked about the power of the heart, and that power has not changed. That power is given to each and every human, to you—not to robots, but you!

Embrace the knowing; that the power we possess with thoughts and emotions changes the photons within our body to whatever we think and feel.

Even if you do not want that power, it is already happening within you. Knowing you are the masters of your own body and mind opens the doorway for you to become masters of the universe. It is said by the ancient mystics that the universe is within us.

We Are a Reflection of Majestic Creation

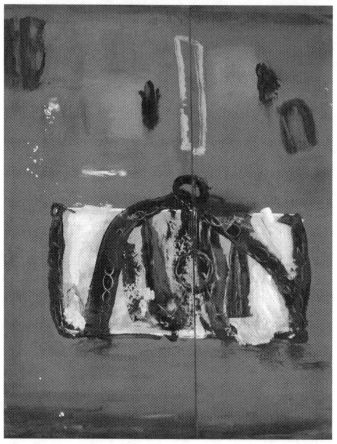

Visualise your dreams coming true. Why not? Everything starts with an idea, a thought.

What is it that you would most love to be or do in your life? Let's set it in action! After all, creative energy is yours, and love is a natural motivator. Yes! Let love be your engine, to light your fire, to ignite your passion for living. Begin by gathering all the material needed around you that will help build your dream.

Masters of the universe, it is your natural right as co creators to bring your full potential into self-actualisation.

Give yourself time, to think about what
it is you would love to become

Your mission is to set your intentions. Then, sit down comfortably on a chair, or lie down if that's what makes you feel more comfortable. Take a few deep breaths, and slowly relax your body with your mind, starting at your toes, travelling slowly upwards, ending at top of your head, repeating to each part 'relax'.

As you slowly relax, allow yourself to visualise a movie screen in front of your mind's eye, as a blank canvas waiting for you to create. When you visualise your dream (from your intentions), feel, see, hear, taste whatever it is you wish to become. Experience it with all the power of receiving it. See yourself in your mind's eye living the dream, whatever that may be for you.

You may be riding a camel in the desert, or you may dream of having a beautiful home. Perhaps you are visualising yourself in a wonderful relationship.

Then let go. By letting go, you are saying to your deeper self, *I allow this to happen, and I trust you.*

Humans are waves of energy in motion, made up of magnetic energy and electric fields, not the computer-Internet field, but a field more powerful and real. This field transmits light energy throughout the universe. And it's alive.

By surfing the web, the Internet, we can check out what mystics of the past have said; scientists have proven that these small particles of light within our body, called photons, mirror our thoughts and emotions, reflecting whatever it is we believe.

Trust in the heart that speaks of eternal love to guide you to this place of dynamic energy that radiates fields of all possibilities. It's through your own heart that you can change your conditioning from the past, which no longer serves your purpose.

What we believe creates what is happening in our physical world right now.

Believe in Yourself

You are the masters of your world; it's your destiny. What you feed your thoughts, your body, and your cells is up to you. Hippocrates, the father of medicine, said, "Let thy food be thy medicine and thy medicine be thy food."

Think of a car: if you feed it with low-grade petrol and oil, it will not run well. It is the same with your mind and body: what you feed into it gives you the energy to stay alive, in health and wakefulness. Feed it well, my friend. Strive for excellence.

Dreams Are Happening!

Like the tide of the ocean, possibilities are waves of energy moving in and out of consciousness, coming from the universal intelligence, waiting to be plucked out of the air, to be nurtured, and brought to fruition, by whomever is willing and receptive to take them. Action must follow.

By utilising your mind's eye, align with your soul, and imagine yourself fast forwarded two years in time; you'll be amazed with the white screen technique, for when you look back at those two years, you will have exceeded all expectations. Because you are not working alone.

Masters of the universe, you are co creators with your higher self. Who are you? What are you? You are—*we* are—co creators with the universe. To attain mastery of the universe is to have self-mastery.

It Starts and Ends with You

We Are Our Own Creators

Everything in your life is what you have created, be it good or bad. You can achieve, live your dream, and be anything you want; it is your life to change and create.

Let It Be with Awareness from Now On

Be aware of your thoughts, emotions, and feelings; are they positive or negative? Our beliefs produce our reality. Our negative beliefs can be patterns that bind us.

> *"Your vision will become clear only*
> *when you look into your heart.*
> *Who looks outside, dreams.*
> *Who looks inside, awakens."*
>
> —Carl Jung

Take responsibility, watch, and focus your attention on what you are thinking. Observing thought patterns and what arises inside you is a good working tool. Being the observer of your thoughts allows you to detach from them. You can choose to think positive beliefs. Believe in the directions of your dreams.

> *"Watch your thoughts; they become words.*
> *Watch your words; they become actions.*
> *Watch your actions; they become habits.*
> *Watch your habits; they become character.*
> *Watch your character; it becomes your destiny."*
>
> —*Lao Tzu*

As you become aware, it will shift your consciousness to a better level of understanding and awareness. As humans, when we feel in our hearts the emotion of love rather than fear, is that not more powerful? Would that not give us a natural protection from fear?

As masters of light and love, know that particles are within and around you, are constantly moving, changing themselves, and our thoughts have an incredible power over these particles. You are the master! Why not align with your divine self? Whatever you think and do naturally affects your physical world, your environment, and the people in it.

Whether you choose this mission or not, you participate in changing particles of energy. Your focus and your intention have strong effects in creating your world and the world around you. Bring awareness to your thought patterns. Breathe in newness, breathe out worn out thoughts.

You do not have to be in competition with others. You are a unique individual, so there is no need to be better than anyone else.

Only You Have Control over You

It is your life, your decision, your choice; you are in the driver's seat. Only you have control over you! You have a power within you that nothing in the universe can take from you. Our choices guide us. We have the power to choose peace over war.

Mastering others is strength.
Mastering yourself is true power.

Lao Tzu

Desire to do, for you, the best you can for you. You are the master of your destiny; nobody can take that position. It is yours.

It Belongs to You and You Alone

You cannot control what others may think, say, or do. That is not your place. What you say, think, and do, however, is entirely yours to own. If you allow others to think for you or control you, then it is your loss.

Your mission, should you wish to accept it, is to accept yourself and learn self-mastery. Focus on your heart space. Concentrate on your feelings.

That doesn't mean to say we cannot listen, look, or learn from what others have achieved, said, or created. After all, we stand on the shoulders of those who have come before us. Humanity marches forward; we can look back and learn from the mistakes and gifts given from others. For example, the global progress of social media, be it a gift or a curse, is here to stay. Accepting that, we live in both a positive and a negative world.

> *Knowing others is wisdom,*
> *knowing yourself is Enlightenment.*
>
> *Lao Tzu*

Sometimes, it costs a little pain to change; it's okay, cause it's just letting you know you're alive and kicking arse!

The twenty-first century is a technology age, in which artificial intelligence is rapidly advancing and taking precedence. We are at the development stage, where we will not only ride the first wave into the next century but also see mankind riding in automotive cars with no drivers, and in all probability, in the next twenty years, we will see flying cars. As seen in the tv series 'The Jetsons'.

Look up on the Internet "Watson," IBM's computer brain; it's just the beginning of what computers are capable of becoming. These types of computers will take a larger role, more and more, within our society. They will take the jobs of mundane repetitive work from us, thank the heavens! Computers do these kinds of jobs better; we humans find repetitive work boring anyway; we make so many mistakes when our minds go to sleep or drift off into la la land. Machines follow a mathematical formula, a repetitive pattern; this makes it a positive move for humanity. Let the robots do all the mundane work so we can concentrate on being truly creative.

We are at the beginning of this wave, and the youth of today must tackle this challenge. This movement will grow and mature into a second and third wave of this technology age.

Therefore, your mission is to grow positively with this wave, to own collaborative relationships with robots, androids, and humans alike. Become a better person with mental stamina each and every day, apply yourself to learn more about emotional intelligence, and improve your physical well-being.

Digital media and computer growth continues at a rapid pace to bring profound change in our lives, in all areas of societies on the globe, particularly in our economic environment. Are you going to have to fight over jobs with computers? It's in your hands whether it turns out to benefit you.

We need to be ready and have the emotional maturity to take the full force of this exponential movement, as it begins to take its

First Baby Steps

To be truly successful in life is not about making money or having material things, but at the end of your life, it will be in the knowing that you made the best of your life and lived its full potential.

When you leave this earth plane, what you take with you is your character and peace of mind. When you can say to yourself, you have done well and given your best, that's success.

It's Not What Others Have Perceived Is Best for You

Play

You enjoy life by being happy.

Masters of the universe, be happy.

You are beautiful souls.

Be not afraid to let your conscience be a guide and listen to the small voice within.

It knows you more intimately than anyone else can.

Change your limited beliefs to potential and change the world around you.

Your mission is to think for yourself.
Reflect on your actions.

Remember the three Ls: Look, Learn, Listen. Decide what it is that you want to achieve. You can achieve anything, and be anything you want to be, within the bounds of universal laws.

As masters of the universe, the dream is yours to create. There are endless possibilities and limitless abundance to be had. First you need to visualise. Dream a little dream. Remember, your movie screen is a blank canvas for you to dare to dream.

Dare to Dream

Become the Dream

If You Can Dream It, You Can Do It

Being young gives you the ability to experiment with what you want, and sometimes just experiencing what you *don't* want, gives you the understanding of what it is that you *do* want. Remember, everything is connected.

Whatever you want to accomplish, you can achieve step by step. You can stop sometimes to smell the roses, but you can never give up.

Let me share a story with you: My headmaster called me aside when I was at the end of my school years. He said to me, "You can be whatever you want to be: teacher, scientist, doctor, train driver, accountant, designer; all you need to remember is to be persistent."

It works; persistence gets you there in the end. In other words, never give up.

Did you see *The Patriot*, the movie with Mel Gibson? What made an impression on me was the repeated phase, "stay the course."

Stay the Course

Focus on your goals.   Focus on your purpose.

Life has a tendency to knock you down, but we have to learn to get back up and continue on the path. Persistence and patience are keys to open the door to success. Your mission is to get back up, dust yourself off, and start all over again. Because you'll benefit, flying high on the wings of love

Other people in your life may tell you that you're not good enough to do this, to achieve that, why bother with this, you can't do that, and so on. This can disconnect you from living your life, your dream. It can make feel unworthy, separated from love.

When you perceive that you belong to the Divine Mother and Father first and last, you will experience a sense of worthiness. You are loved, and you belong.

"All knowledge has its origins in our perceptions."
— *Leonardo Da Vinci*

Believe, breath in Your Soul, and Know
the Story of Your Heart

Masters of the universe, true love is holy. Live in love. If you
feel others have hurt you, say to yourself, *I'm sorry, forgive
me* or, *I forgive you.*

Send that pain with light and love out to the universe
and let the Divine Mother take care of it. Then let it go.
By repeating this mantra, you can transmute unwanted
negative thoughts instantly; this clears your headspace and
sets you free for action.

If you cannot cope with issues, take a risk and see a
counsellor. There are many beautiful people out there in
the world who have found their calling and are willing to
give service.

Be Kind to Yourself, Connect Within to Your Inner Self

And don't hesitate to give a little kindness to someone else.
It goes a long way to your spiritual bank account.

Scientists have discovered, from what they call
entanglement, that when particles are split, these particles
don't separate their connection; they communicate, and
they behave as one. In other words, when protons are
separated by distance, they are still connected as a whole.
Their memory is intact. Now that's natural intelligence,
thats your natural birthright.

Somewhere in the Maze

of Human Emotions

Deep within You Is a Spring of Light

a Place of Peace,

a

Divine Matrix of Love

That Is Unconditional

Your higher self, is connected to Source connected to that which loves you ... and is unconditional, eternal, and forever Love.

Although you may have moments of feelings so alone, in truth, you are not.

Your Mission Is to Build Resilience

"The nitrogen in our DNA, the calcium in our teeth, the iron in our blood, the carbon in our apple pies were made in the interiors of collapsing stars. We are made of starstuff."

- Carl Sagan, Cosmos

Harry Potter Magic

Our spirit is made in light; we are made from the colours of the rainbow, be it blue, orange, yellow, red, rose, white. It's no fantasy! Thoughts travels at the speed of light, in an instant; yes, thoughts have wings. We can heal others from the power of thought, transferring love and light into the atmosphere, from our hearts, focused on the individual you wish to help.

Because humans live in a sea of emotions, we can and do become vulnerable. We can be uncertain. We can doubt.

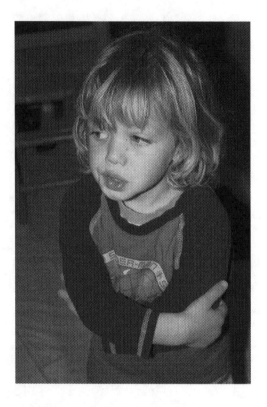

When we feel doubt, shame, or fear, our light becomes dim, and we live in the shadow self. We live disconnected from our authentic selves and to others. We struggle for understanding and enlightenment. It is in this struggle where we learn about compassion; to understand pain and to understand others in pain, we learn empathy. We are not alone.

We are not robots, because we do experience emotional pain and suffer enormously. It is a human condition, so don't take it personally.

Embrace this condition, as it's what songs are sung about, what stories are written about, and what great artists wring their passion from.

Be not afraid to love one another, to connect, to invest in relationships, that may or may not work out. Be brave and take a risk. We will all experience feeling vulnerable; it is a trait we should not run away from but embrace as our deliverance. Something good comes out of the darkness. In other words, eventually it can be transformed into something beautiful.

> *A beautiful thing never gives so much pain*
> *as does failing to hear and see it.*
>
> *Michelangelo*

Life is a challenge. Your mission is to face that challenge. As humans, we cannot avoid things that happen in our lives that are not in our power to control. For example, we may experience the death of a loved one, people getting sick, loss of jobs, separation, moving to another country, or seeing our friends with addictive habits. These things may hurt, but hey, we have to move through it. There is no need to pretend that we are not hurt or vulnerable. It's okay.

However, to turn a blind eye is not the way; we must work our way through the process of pain and uncertainty. Because as the ancients mystic masters tell us, "Our emotions are valuable." If we try to block out the unhappy feelings, we block out other parts of ourselves that are so precious: our feelings of joy and happiness and growth.

It's okay to go through feelings of rejection: He (or she) doesn't love me anymore. I feel unworthy and unwanted. Look at those feelings, understand them, share them with others, talk about them, then let them go. Don't judge them.

Let them go, don't hold on to them. Release them. Blow them into the wind, then let go and move on. In the end, you will experience more respect within yourself and create a harmony called inner peace.

"So Divinely is the world organised that every one of us,
in our place in time,
is in balance with everything else."
—Johann Wolfgang von Goethe

Remember, as human beings, we are working towards the ultimate perfection, and we make mistakes as a way of learning. You are still worthy of that universal love and belonging to the Divine. That's a given. Your mission is to practice being grateful for this sense of belonging.

Thanking the universe just for being alive acts as positive energy, like waves, moving outward, like the rippling of a pebble thrown into a still turquoise lake. Joy and happiness will follow close on your heels, like baby cubs following their mama.

Can you see artificial intelligence giving thanks for moments during day-to-day living? Gratitude is something not to be taken lightly.

In the beginning, God created a story … so the story goes.
The story of Creation.
Throughout human history. Stories told around campfires.
Stories told, written, painted, sung, chanted, rituals passed down through the ages.

Ancient Knowledge Woven in Mythology

Egyptology, Aborigine dreamtime, Greek mythology, Chinese mythology—the list is endless. And then there are stories told to us as children.

But what about your story? Are you going to be the hero of your story? Why or why not?

Your story is unique. Your soul is unique. Share the story of your authentic self to the world, and the mosaic of life will change. Your story influences everything around you. Let yourself be seen deeply. Find what you love to do, and love your life with all of your might. Robots are programmed; they don't have to strive to towards goals. Discover your reason for living. Give yourself time to dream!

Reality Is Whatever You Perceive It To Be

True success comes when you are following your greater purpose.

Your mission is to find your purpose for living. It may be to be kind and loving towards others. It may be to learn or inspire others through art, making music, or science. It may be to be a leader, nurse, or teacher in your community. These wonderful women, and many others, have dedicated their lives to making a difference, not only in the world, but to children's education and future.

It may be to be a beautiful mother or father.

It may be to care for the animals, the plants, the planet.

In other words, it matters not how simple or how grand your reason for living is, it's that you have the focus and motivation each day to be counted and an understanding that you will wake up each day loving yourself because you have a purpose for living. You can make a difference in the world. Obstacles become challenging in a positive way, games to puzzle over as you find different ways of overcoming them.

Your mission is to feel good about who you are, count your blessings, pat yourself on the back each day for achieving (no matter how little), as a job well done. Be passionate that you are alive and on a mission, your mission, your purpose, your dream.

If you don't feel passionate towards living, say no to what you are doing. And look again. Ask within. What is it that you would love to become? Remember, dreams are powerful tools and motivators. Believe in yourself. Working with your inner self assists you in a more authentic way, in finding what you want. Have a deep interest in your purpose.

It's the desire and the passion that make you want to rock, to work, to progress, to simply enjoy what you are doing.

Breathe in the air.

Connect

Communicate with yourself, with others, and with your world, and in participating, focus on your dream for working and living.

One way to become in tune with yourself is listening intently to music as a positive activity. Engage in it totally, the impact of listening with all of your being. Research has shown this has a fuller impact and brings you into your soul.

Music Is a Friend for Life

Share it with the world and your friends. Participate in this receiving and giving, this breath of sound. Live the spirit of music within. The universe is a vibrating harmonic motion. Your heart has a rhythmic drumbeat. Listen to the rhythm of life, and dance to it.

If you listen within, you may hear the harmony of the spheres.

A Hologram of Music

Be in the rhythm of your heart, in harmony with your dreams, and experience your friend in music. This is where humankind has precedence over artificial intelligence. Our soul responds to music, to many different types of melodies, and if that is where you want to spend time to express yourself, go for it; there may even be a job out there for you. Remember that old saying: Practice makes perfect.

When you are courting a nice girl an hour seems like a second.
When you sit on a red-hot cinder a second seems like an hour.
That's relativity.

Albert Einstein

To be masters of the universe is to respect yourself. By respecting yourself, you will respect your planet and all living creatures that rely on our guardianship.

We Have to Put in to Get Out What We Want in Life
Being a Co-Creator of the Universe Is About Our Participation

Another old saying rings true: "God helps those who help themselves." Let your environment reflect your inner thoughts, with what it is that you desire in life. If there is something you don't want, you have the power to change it. You have the power of the universe behind you when you work in harmony with natural laws.

You may ask, What are these universal laws and how do they affect little ol' me? Newton's law tells us that every action has a reaction or response. As you sow, so shall you reap. As you give, so shall you receive. What does that mean, and how does it relate to you?

Your mission—should you desire to be a sexy, intelligent person—is to understand you are not superior or inferior. You just are.Your mission is to understand and work in harmony with these wonderful universal laws.

Laws are happening all around us. They are not the laws that we are subject to within our community or family, like stopping at the red traffic light.
Laws, as in, Why doesn't the sun fall down? How does it know to rhythmically rise every morning?

> *This is one of man's oldest riddles. How can the independence of human volition be harmonised with the fact that we are integral parts of a universe which is subject to the rigid order of nature's laws?*
>
> *-Max Plank*

These laws are greater than human law. It is natural law, commanded at the beginning of creation. Always constructive, even when it appears not to be. It is the manifestation of cosmic energy and order. Nature is divine in its essence, not supernatural but natural.

Let's Call Them Grand Laws of the Universe

We witness the push and pull of life, the attraction and repulsion within these natural laws; for example, the moon pulls the ocean tides in and out each day.

For self-mastery, it's naturally more beneficial for everyone to work within these laws. Meaning, the law of attraction pertains to what we put out, we get back.
In other words, what we are thinking and feeling is what we attract to ourselves.
Your mission is to bring your emotions, feelings, and thoughts into alignment with the greater self within, so as

to experience harmony within as a oneness. Then you truly begin to attract what it is you desire.

Your greater purpose is easy when you can listen to your inner self, your intuitive voice, and react from that space. Grab your happiness, and radiate love and peace from your heart.

Sometimes others do not participate, and that's okay. As long as you know what you are giving out, you're sure to benefit greatly.

Let me share with you Blake Mycoskie's story. After observing children without shoes in Argentina, he created TOMS Shoes; through his compassion, he's given over ten million pairs of shoes to kids in need. This led to a very successful business, within the law of giving and receiving. He didn't stop there when he saw another need: eyewear. In his inspirational book, *Start Something that Matters*, Mycoskie said, "When you have a memorable story about who you are and what your mission is, your success no longer depends on how experienced you are or how many degrees you have or who you know. A good story transcends boundaries, breaks barriers, and opens doors. It is a key not only to starting a business but also to clarifying your own personal identity and choices."

Our personal identity and choice contributes to the intricate mosaic pattern we call life.

Your Power Is in Your Intentions

What type of energy are you putting out? This energy comes back to you and contributes to everything else around you. Loving and respecting your life brings that energy back to you, breathing in light and breathing out release.

Feeling this natural rhythm surrounding you and within you. Feeling your authentic self, now, that's true value for money. Remember, life is filled with tremendous possibilities.

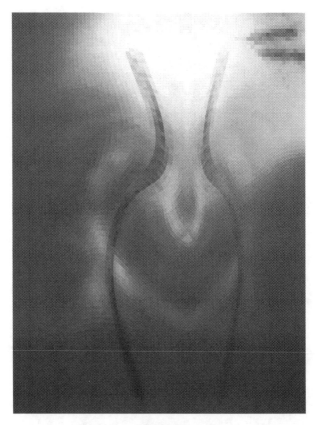

Always

It could be said that we are a product of our environment and our educational system. Nevertheless, your authentic self is with you wherever you go, whatever you become, and whatever you do. It's within you, and if you need to change and grow, it is you who must do the changing, not the places, the friends, or the family members, but you. Okay, so there may be old thoughts, outdated patterns of behaviour, that weigh you down.

Robots won't have the capacity to do, think, and act as we do, simply because scientists cannot create spirit; it's what makes humans such complex beings. The challenge is until we learn what it is we are meant to be learning, history, our story, will repeat itself over and over again.

For example, when a movie is made, lots of what is shot is edited or deleted.
How do we cut that reel of unwanted patterning that prevents us from having new ones? By looking at and taking responsibility for our thought patterns, we can change them to produce constructive positive outcomes. Transformation for change is ours; similar to a caterpillar changing into a beautiful butterfly, we can transform ourselves now.

> *"Do not wait to strike till the iron is hot,*
> *but make it hot by striking."*
> —*William Butler Yeats*

Your mission is to own your authentic self. It's the first step in becoming a master of the universe. It's okay to be you, and if there is a part of you that needs changing, change it. Take responsibility for what is in your life, and that will give you the power to change what feels wrong.

It takes work to change and grow, but the results are rewarding, and true happiness does follow. Because the truth is, you can only experience true success when your actions are in line with your greater purpose.

*"Most people choose to believe that God communicates
in special ways and only with special people ... All
people are special, and all moments are golden."*
— *Neale Donald Walsch,*
Conversations with God, Book 1

When you use your intuitive self, you tune yourself to the best information possible from the Source, that higher intelligence within. Give trust for its guidance; your higher self knows your deeper story.

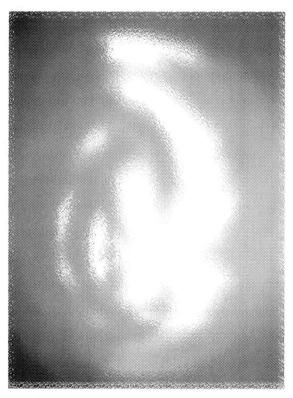

Our Soul's Journey

In all probability, artificial intelligence may be programmed in reference to values. What is it that you value? Masters of the universe, the first rule is to value yourself. You are precious to your Divine Mother and Father.

Do not allow another person to take parts of you. People can take away your self-worth, your self-esteem, or you may have unintentionally given away some part of yourself. Perhaps, from childhood conditioning, if you allow people to have power over you, they will take it. Perhaps you recognise missing fragments within yourself, from others reflecting back to you like a mirror image.

Comparing the difference between robots and being human is that, as people, we sometimes can give away the most precious things we love, perhaps by wanting to control relationships or compulsive habits to drink or do drugs or even video gaming. We can give away our precious family life. Sadly, addictions create havoc.

Fight for the right to bring wholeness back into your life. Others do not have the right to disrespect you. There is a great power in respecting yourself; it gives you the space to think for yourself and to be who you truly are, without taking from others. People will then learn not to walk all over you, but take what you are giving and give you something back that has value.

Respect Follows Respect,   Love Begets Love

We live in a shared world, so when you are in conversation with another, use your eyes with genuine warmth. Give each moment your undivided attention; studies show significantly greater feelings of respect and kindliness are remembered on a subconscious level. A sense of humour goes down well, try a nod and a wink, that always gets them.

In other words, simply saying hello to another person, acknowledging him or her like a bosom companion and allowing warmth to come from your heart that is overflowing with love, gives something of true value that doesn't cost a cent.

My father was like that, so warm and generous, a storyteller who hooked people in with loving eyes and an open smile.

Then his words would flow and send strangers into fits of laughter. When it is given from that heart space, it is free and comes with abundance. We reflect ourselves in others.

It sounds easy, but it's not. It takes mastery.

Be comfortable in your space, allow the space of friendship with another to grow, and experience the diversity of each other, to enjoy and share ideas.

Recognise Your Spiritual Connection with Others

In return, you create a new friend and add more depth and richness to both lives.

Obstacles will be cut in half, and you will flow with abundance of positive coincidences.

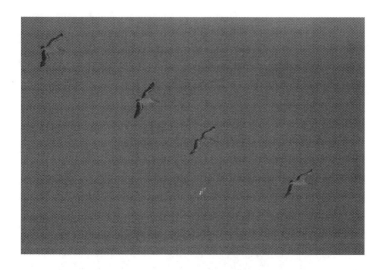

Masters of the universe, you are created as a spark of the Divine. Yes, our bodies are made up of 75 percent fluid, yet we radiate an aura of energy because we are also made up of electromagnetic energy. Everything in the universe is vibrating energy, vibrating at a different rate of frequency.

Remember, we are made up of photons of light. Tiny packets of light energy. Our bodies vibrate these as waves of energy. The awesome thing about photons is that they change. When our DNA is introduced, they align themselves with the DNA, as seen in the experiment called the phantom effect, discovered by Russian scientists Gariaev and Poponin. When the DNA is taken out, the photons act like they are still connected. The memory remains.

Soul memories lives within our very being. The universe is connected to us, from the beginning of Creation. DNA can change your emotions, and there is proof that feelings of peace and love can relax the DNA.

Artificial intelligence does not have the same genetic makeup, no flesh and blood to deal with; the material could be metallic, until something like human skin is developed.

The invention of skin … mmmmmm, difficult.

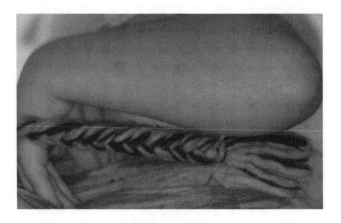

Skin has a relationship with touch and feeling; it covers the blood and guts, the brain, the stomach, the kidneys, the liver, and so forth. It protects the intelligent systems working naturally within the body. We tend to take these for granted. Be grateful; positive thoughts keep you healthy and feeling on top of your game.

Questions are being asked such as:

- Will artificial intelligence overpower humans?
- Can robots become more sophisticated than humans?
- Will they outthink us?

I interviewed a young man who started his own technology business when he left school fifteen years ago. I asked him where he thought technology is now, in the year January 2016, and where it is heading.

Gabriel Craven, director of ITG Technology, Australia, said he thinks that a new type of human will emerge. He had this to say: "Technology today is at its infancy stage; if we look back in history to the invention of flight, technology is at the stage of flying kites before the Wright Brothers even thought of inventing the plane. Today, technology is at its most exciting time in history; in the same breath, it's at its worst time. It's growing at such a rate that it's becoming uncontrollable now. Humans are immersing themselves in technology; deeper and deeper, they dive into the abyss. Robotics will integrate into humans creating the next stage of human evolution: the Cyborg, part human, part machine."

Today, this technology still relies on humans; without human interaction, technology will die. We can't and won't be able to stop its progress; therefore, technology will get to a stage where it will no longer require any human interaction, and it will become its own living entity.

The next stage, which is the most frightening for humanity, is artificial intelligence. With AI, humans will no longer be the dominant species in the universe. This living entity will know everything about us and have our centuries of knowledge in a matter of seconds.

Question: If we are going to program robots (AI), isn't it important that we program them with ethics and integrity? Gabriel replied, "What can be learned can be unlearned. True, AI will be able to reprogram themselves. AI will start out like us individuals, then it will grow into one entity, one consciousness, which is something humans have been unable to achieve.

"Imagine every human brain working as one to solve a problem; imagine what can be achieved. This is what this living entity has the possibility of doing in a blink of an eye."

Question: What about feeling of love and hate? Gabriel said, "As soon as they start thinking for themselves, as a human, I can only guess. They will know what feelings are; it is whether they choose to use them. They may only use them to interact with us; what I'm trying to say is, feelings are optional."

Question: Why should we create something that has the possibility to be destructive?

Gabriel answered, "Humans have always created things that destroy, for control. Humanity today is losing their grip on controlling technology. Look at the Internet. Governments attempt to control it but it's too late; it's out of control."

Question: How does this affect humanity?

Gabriel said, "We will continue to immerse ourselves in technology until it controls us. Everything we do will be on, and controlled by, the internet. Soon, people will have the opportunity to plug their brains directly into the internet. In other words, they no longer need a phone or computer to connect themselves to the internet.

Our communication will change, how we socialise will change, our realities will change, and we will no longer be humans. Humanity will become the very technology that it created, and we will lose what makes us humans. In terms of universal intelligence, there are forces in the universe that are greater than humanity."

Question: Are you saying this technology is created by this other force?

Gabriel replied, "Yes, short answer to what I am saying is, there's a driving force of life beyond evolution. Life doesn't gamble on one species, or it would have left the table when the dinosaurs died out. Life has a plan, and it's driven humans into a symbiotic relationship with technology; at some point in the future, this relationship will end what we call being human. Bio-tech will be the final stage."

It has become appallingly obvious
that our technology
has exceeded our humanity.
-Albert Einstein

There you have it: Texting and even the iPhone will be obsolete; we need only to project what we want, through our thoughts. We can merge with technology insomuch as the neurones in our brain will respond instantaneously to technology's computerised information, to anything and everything that has been created.

I respect what Gabriel had to say, and on reflection, AI is just that, artificial; on the other hand, we are complex human beings. Let's differentiate between the two, for clarity's sake.

Why can't humankind accept differences, love one another, and live in peace? Does our cultural upbringing have anything to do with our differences? Due to the growth of technology and the internet, understanding cultural diversity is important. Cross-cultural communication is an education in itself. In today's global world, understanding how people communicate from a wide range of cross-cultural backgrounds and beliefs requires new communication strategies. The diversity of difference brings difficulty, in that our perception and cultural differences do create barriers and new challenges.

I like differences; personally, I think they are what makes the world go round—the spice of life and all that. I sometimes wonder why some humans want to make everything like them, the same.

Cultures are important in that they provide rules of how we conduct ourselves, how to behave, how to be a good human being. Sounds so simple when such cultures do provide people with ways of communicating effectively with one another and ways of interpreting the world around them. The rules differ from culture to culture, and I suppose that's what makes complexity. Maybe it's because each culture has dissimilar frames of references into how we should be, act, see.

Robots are made; human beings develop and grow from babyhood, experiencing the world and interpreting what they see, believe, hear, and learn, each from a different cultural perspective. Added to the mix is how we differ in our nonverbal communication also.

I spent time in the south of France, which gave me a greater understanding of how much nonverbal communication is expressed differently across a wide range of cultures. On top of learning the language itself is the difficulty of understanding the hidden nuisances that nonverbal communication conveys, which is learnt from the cradle to the grave and passed on from generation to generation.

We don't intentionally want to offend the other person we are trying to communicate with, yet in our ignorance, we can. Gestures with hands or eye contact can be understood differently, as can how one talks with his or her eyes or stands close to the other person with arms folded in front of him or her. Eye contact, in particular towards women, could be viewed as sexual, yet not giving a person eye contact could be classed as rude. Spanish and Italian cultures like to use their hands in expressing themselves, and in other cultures, extreme gesturing can take on a whole new meaning. Our emotional response is expressed differently; in some cultures, people openly express their feelings, and it's okay to cry your heart out, to shout and talk loudly, or to get angry. Pointing your finger at someone to give directions can be inappropriate in China, yet normal in Australia.

Can AI have the same input and responses? The potential with humans, let alone robots, for misunderstanding from translating is considerable.

Our lack of understanding how other cultures relate with these nonverbal cues, as well as not speaking the language, makes cross-cultural communication a problem. Nevertheless, we can make it a positive test of our abilities for understanding and learning, knowing it is needed more than ever in our expanding global world. There are so many different points of views, ways of looking, philosophies, idealism, belief systems, and who is right and who is wrong. Wouldn't it make a difference if we decided, as a human race, to accept the differences and get on with it? To make an effort of living together with our own cultural beliefs: I respect your space, if you respect my space. Would it be more educational if schools taught nonviolent communication, so we can get on with living and respecting differences?

Australia is a fine example of a multicultural society trying to live in peace and harmony. I say good luck to them; it's sad to see the different cultures in the world and all the different languages which are dying out.

How we view the world, and hear the world, has an effect on our brain, as well as our psyche.

Researcher Dr Karl Pribram of Stanford University has said that the human brain records information in a holographic way. (Holography is from Greek origin meaning 'complete writing.') Information is intelligently stored over a family of brain neurones, not in any one particular small group of neurones, and that the brain is continuously engaged in correlation processes.

If you cut a hologram into very small pieces, it still retains the recognisable image as the whole object. Each part contains some information of the whole.

Each individual human brain acts as a holographic part of a total hologram. That's amazingly sophisticated. Human consciousness simultaneous mirrors our thoughts, feelings, and emotions, on many levels holographically. It is done. Now! In this moment!

Robots don't have a body created like humans, where diseases happen and the body dies; will they end up being superior to humans? On the other hand, will genetic engineering eliminate disease, with artificial intelligent implants, like bionic eyes and ears?

Scientists have come up with precise molecular scissors for cutting and pasting DNA. Known as the CRISPR, these scissors may be used to correct genetic diseases such as HIV. This technology can create designer babies and play around with the DNA of our future. Do they have the right to do this? Masters of the universe, think about which type of world you want to live in: natural or designer made?

Are we at the beginning of creating a new breed of humans? The desire to assist people who have lost an arm or a leg has led scientists to create half-human and half-robotic people, which in turn creates the desire to make robots more human. They don't need to breathe air. Not having organs doesn't necessarily mean that it's going to be a metal machine. We will have nanobots, which are biotech, biology, therefore, living creatures that can be put in the brain or nervous system of humans in the future.

In the end, we could be asking ourselves the question, what comes first, the chicken or the egg, the robot or the child? For example, scientists have created a smart chip to put in the part of the brain that retains long-term memory, to enable a child to be smarter. Is having access to this area of the brain worth making your sisters and brothers smarter?

At present, most humans perceive their earthly parents as a reflection of an expectation of the Divine Mother and Father. Deep within ourselves, we have a perceived notion of the male and female function, and how we see our divine relationship within this role. These perceptions are revealed in why we chose our parents.

Before we entered this earth plane, our souls were whole, created with both the masculine and feminine. As individuals, we try to identify with that wholeness, even on a subconscious level. For example, if the masculine is taken away, we look for it in others, to bring that balance into our lives.

As individuals grow, they have periods of self-realisation. What will be the consequences of having a smart chip planted in the brain, in terms of personal growth?
There is no indication that it will make a child more emotionally mature or rational enough to make unselfish choices for the betterment of humanity. Are we going to be fighting for our survival just to be human, as people merge with artificially intelligence, or will our soul emerge as victorious? Where is all this technological growth leading to?

In the progress of the industrial age, with the invention of cars, the question was asked, "Do we really need it?" The answer, then, was that you can't stop progress.
The cutting of the rainforest in the Amazon is an example of so-called progress. Basically, we know that trees give out oxygen, and without oxygen, we as humans will die. Essentially, on a soul level, we have a desire to see their beauty. Symbolically, the tree plays a role in human history.

Some would say that today we are experiencing huge
storms on the planet from the destructive acts of progress,
as nature endeavours to balance herself. Lucky individuals
do help by caring for this delicate balance of plant, animal,
and human life living on this awesome planet called
Earth. Would artificial intelligence show such concern? Yet
progress we must, and as masters of the universe, the future
lies in our hands. The way I see it, there's lots of work to be
done to bring all the levels of intelligence into balance.

We can help by simply looking out for one another and
caring for the animals on the planet, such as the state of the
polar bears, who find their home melting away, day by day.

As individuals, we perceive and make decisions based on
our beliefs and conditioning. When we experience negative
energy and it stays unresolved, it can lay deep within our
subconscious and create negative patterns in our lives.
Negative energy happens, yet how can it benefit us? What is
it we need to learn from this experience?

Most times we are not in the heart, for the heart has no
judgement. The heart sees through the eyes of divine
love. Nevertheless, we cannot bypass negative energy
experienced; we need to work through the situation. When
we do, as a result, it releases ideas out of the subconscious
mind, freeing us to live in peace.

When something causes you pain, it's nothing to do with liking it; you need to be strong enough to embrace the experience, bless it, and acknowledge it. Work through it. Yes, it hurts. Yet you need to let go of this hurt eventually; otherwise, it's like a poison that leaks into your mind, body, and emotions.

Giving thanks to a person who hurt you is not an easy thing to do; nevertheless, we do need to release the experience. Send it out to the universe on the wings of light. As a result, it doesn't clutter up the subconscious mind. Replace it with acceptance; all will work out.

One day your heart will take you to your lover.
One day your soul will carry you to the beloved.
Don't get lost in your pain,
know that one day your pain will become your cure.
— *Rumi*

Your spiritual mother and father love you. It's true, their love is unconditional. Having this belief is a positive. Knowing that they belong in your heart is a beautiful thing, and it is a gift that brings beauty into your living.

"If you believe you can, you probably can. If you believe you won't, you most assuredly won't. Belief is the ignition switch that gets you off the launching pad."
—*Denis Waitley*

Nature Reflects Beauty

Do not forget, the fabric of the universe is a living conscious entity, bigger than us mere mortals. (Good word, "mortal," meaning the body at death goes back to the earth, and the spirit back to its creator.) It's up to you to learn from nature and work in harmony for the good of the whole. Although you are not always aware of this invisible landscape, it is there, a pulsating essence of energy vibrating on many levels. This heavenly/earth mind is conscious intelligence.

Our planetary systems, right down to getting up in the morning and eating our breakfast, all follow a rhythmic pattern of imperceptible energy. As individuals, we all have the ability to be psychic and can be sensitive enough to feel this energy. Not like AI, who are artificially programmed, but through our birthright as divine beings, we have this ability mapped out in our DNA.

Feelings of love, compassion, and forgiveness have an effect on this incredible universal web of light energy. It's so easy to forget what's in our hearts when we suffer pain. Nevertheless, love is not pain.

> *A Heart filled with Love*
> *Is like a Phoenix*
> *that no cage can imprison.*
>
> — *Rumi*

We live alongside a dynamic, visible, and invisible intelligent universe, and we are like ants, so busy following the leader, following the glitter of the advertising world, that at times that we lose sight of what really matters. There is a persistent preoccupation in society for the acquisition of consumer goods, lest you think you are missing out.

Be not a slave but a master of the universe. Free yourself from the shopping merry-go-round, reconnect to that deeply authentic part of yourself, and see this cultural conditioning as something you can successfully navigate rather than something that consumes you.

Find the Balance Within

Staying confidently connected to your authentic self matters. When we boil everything down to empty space, we discover, in fact that space is not empty.

There Is No Empty Space

Rather, there is a field of energy that glues all energy together. We can't see it; similar to cyberspace or the Internet; we cannot discern it, but we utilise it. However, unlike the Internet, the soul knows. Our spiritual web, or connections, are far more real and long lasting. Some may call it the divine matrix, the all-knowing eye of God.

Because of the past, because of conditioning, you may carry lots of fear. Love or fear create feelings. Using love instead of fear brings better results for your confidence and self-worth. Breathe, with awareness, the power of love into your thoughts and emotions, and bring unity to your heart. All is one. Awareness of your inner self brings you closer to web of light that spreads instantly to your point of *intention*.

Confidence Brings Peace

We live on a planet of love. Love is universal. On Facebook, we see lots of images of animals and how much love they express to their owners and friends. We see love being portrayed in a smile from the interactions of all races on the planet, be it Chinese, English, Japanese, or French, from the desire to photograph ourselves through selfies now. Maybe, one day, even from AI?

Creative people have made movies, like *Ex Machina, Tomorrowland,* and *Blade Runner,* of artificial intelligence learning the language of love. But as humans, we know how much joy it can bring and the flip side how much pain we can endure in the name of love.

Nevertheless, the language of love is a verbal and nonverbal universal language; it works in favour of whatever action you want in your life. What do you hold in your heart? Is it love or fear? What is that natural force, the glue the weaves the Universe together? Is it love? Is it love that I'm feeling?

"Be happy in the moment; that's enough. Each moment is all we need, not more."
—*Mother Teresa*

There is untapped potential in the mind. The challenge is not to rely on false thinking. When the thought and the emotion become one with the Creator, then you truly have the power to create.

One of the secrets of the universe is imagination. It's a vital key to unlocking your potential. When utilising your imagination you will have the whole force of the universe behind you. There is a diverse richness, a limitless resource waiting gladly, when you open this door within your mind and heart.

The true sign of intelligence is not knowledge but imagination.
-Albert Einstein

Oh, masters of the universe, because the main task of this extraordinary universe, the Grand Architect of the Universe is to create, everything created from humans in this world, be it the past, present, or future, comes from the imagination, from a person's mind—the imagination. There is a limitless pot of gold at the end of this rainbow, in this mysterious realm. Forever waiting to begin something new and continuously filled with endless possibilities.

In our dreams, our imagination goes wild. I remember having a dream. I was sitting on the toilet and reached for the toilet paper, and it turned into money. What did that mean? Now looking back, it was saying that the not-so-nice stuff we go through can be our gold, in that it is where we learn valuable wisdom about life.

Using our imagination seems to be a tool not encouraged in schools, yet it is one of the most valuable gifts you are given from our great Mother and Father.

Think about your future with imagination, and it's amazing how ideas start to flow. You attract to yourself the right cause of action, with one solid vision.

You Are the Architect of You

Creating opportunities for you to succeed can be a dangerous business; fear of failure and loss puts us at risk. But with the willingness to learn, this gives you true potential to win. When asking the universe for anything, be specific as to what you want; the Source we term God needs to see it clearly. Before you project out your desire for assistance from this higher Source, have clarity of purpose. Ask, in the name of your highest good.

When you reunite your human consciousness with the God consciousness within, you are not alone. You can ask specifically for ten helpers or guides, for different parts of your living self, for health, financial prosperity, hope, faith, vision, and so on. Many Cosmic Masters are open to serving mankind, such as Jesus, Buddha, Freya, Mohammed, Osiris, Deganawida, Lao Tse, Hermes, Ba, Chih Nii, and don't forget our heavenly angels.

You have the support of the heavenly hosts of the universe. If you're looking for something long lasting, you're looking in the right place. Tapping into the inner self brings visions, and without visions, nothing much is created. Be brave and face your challenge with confidence.

A key to success is vision.

Quera Apache Prayer

Looking behind, I am filled with gratitude
looking forward, I am filled with vision
Looking upward, I am filled with Strength
Looking within, I discover Peace

Hands Up Those Who Have Experienced Inner Peace

Our souls' personalities are made up of many past lives, each life learning various lessons that our inner selves seek for development of our highest expression. The core part of our souls seek new levels of understanding and growth. Somewhere, somehow, we lost the knowledge and wisdom of this, and in turn, this separated us from our true natures.

I Am a Peacemaker

A few years back, a group of like-minded people came together and consciously decided to meditate on a past-life experience.

I found myself sitting on a horse, looking up at a castle. I was a man, a leader, a strong warrior. I could feel the horse underneath me, breathing. Draped over the horse was a beautiful deep-blue cover. What I found interesting was the focus, the power of the mind, within this man as me. There was an inner stillness. I was motionless; the horse stood still, and everything around me seemed stationary, complete stillness. My focus was clear and undeviating, shaped like a straight arrow going from my mind to the castle, waiting, waiting, waiting in that moment of stillness, for an answer—whether there was to be war or peace.

A couple of years after this insight into one of my past lives, I had a dream.

I was sitting on a horse, looking over a field of devastation. A war had been fought, and many bodies lay mutilated and dead. I was thinking, as I cast my eyes on this killing field, *What a waste of human life.* I vowed then, that was the end of killing for me.

We learn that death is just another doorway, as birth is the doorway or passage to our learning on earth. We have a specific purpose for wanting to come to earth, to experience the light and shadow, the force of gravity, the push and the pull, the sun and the moon.

Through the past, we connect with other wise souls who become our teachers and guides, but ultimately it is our journey to learn, to make mistakes, and to grow.

> *I searched for God and found only myself.*
> *I searched for myself and found only God.*
> —*Sufi Prover*

Sexy Is Being Smart

Learn to accept the polarities of this earth and to balance our energies accordingly.

I received the calling to be a messenger of the greater light when I had a visitation by the Archangel Gabriel, guardian of the garden of paradise. It began in a dream …where else? *Voila!*

There was an immense pure vibration of shimmering golden light. This light shone. It was so magnificent and powerful, words could not describe it. Beyond heaven, I was transported, beyond the boundaries of death, beyond the world of no beginning and no end to feast my eyes upon this glorious living being of heavenly bliss, fire eternal! Astral light of angelic love!

An angel stood at the foot of this great light and did bid me welcome. I, who had dedicated this life to the spiritual realm, glimpsed a moment in the hierarchy of creation. I looked up at this majestic holy being. I was awed. I was stunned. All I managed to gasp, inside my mind was, *Oooh! An angel, Oooh! An angel.*

The being at my side whispered softly in my ear, "Archangel."

Still mesmerised and totally in shock, I just keep saying, "Oooh! An angel. Oooh! An angel," and the voice again spoke softly beside me, saying, "Archangel."

I continued being lost in the sheer overwhelming beauty of this radiant heavenly being floating above me. The angel at my side just waited patiently for the realisation to finally sink into my mind (I was aware of mind, no body, yet I felt whole in myself). Finally, the dawning realisation that this shimmering heavenly creature I was gazing up at was, in fact, more than an angel.

It was an Archangel.

When the full realisation hit me, I immediately experienced a change in energy. I experienced a clear division of the realm of the angels, which was below where I was standing. The most profound experience was seeing that the archangels' world was so far up the scale of the ladder of the heavenly hierocracy. Angels were down the next rung of the ladder.

The hierocracy of angels was diminished in their glory, in comparison to archangels. I was gazing up at another kingdom, another realm altogether. I gulped and thought, *Wow, if that's how far the angels are from this kingdom, earth is a long way down the list.*

Here on earth, an angel is looked up to with such awe and beauty. I had entered a far greater realm, and I was bedazzled. I felt privileged and humbled to have been chosen.

Communion begins, mental telepathy, mind to mind, heart to heart. I become the servant of this great cosmic being. I come to this knowing past wisdom, honouring the laws of the universe. An alchemist, a mystic, acknowledging the power within me, acknowledging the all-seeing eye.

I see before me the perfection of human evolution, seeds to be sown for the next generation of our earthly interesting complex human race.

Listen to your intuition.

As Jose Silva once said, "The reason we are given psychic [intuitive] ability is so we can use it to get information from higher intelligence to find out what we are supposed to do, and how to do it."

Masters of the universe, self-talk, talk to yourself, keep reminding yourself that you are smart because you build your life within, not without. Not on how much you have, but what you are inside.

- Do you think a quick fix is easier?
- Do you buy things to make you feel better?
- Do you take drugs to make you feel good?
- Do you become obsessed with video games?

You're better off facing life head on, with self-talk to aid you. For example, "This is where I am, it's not where I want to be. I am not going to blame anything or anyone; chances are the circumstance evolved through a number of reasons. "What's more important is, how do I get out of the situation, to better myself? What are the steps to take for the solution to resolve itself?

"During this life, many doors will close, and many doors of opportunity will open."

"I am ready to go through these door. I need to be awake and aware when they are presented to me. Nothing is impossible, there are no limits to what I want in life when I am at one with my inner self."

Would you say to future robots, "Put your money where your mouth is, and be in harmony with what you say think and do"?

It's not likely.

Say to yourself on a daily basis, "I am grateful for all that is. I am grateful that I am love. I am grateful for this beautiful planet. I am grateful for my visible and invisible guides, like my angels. I am grateful, as they bring grace and inspiration into my life. I am grateful for my connection with divine light and universal intelligence.

Be generous with yourself and others, be kind, and give love from the heart. Ask for nothing in return, knowing you are fulfilling a natural law; as you give, so shall you receive. It's an awesome feeling.

Forgive yourself and others around for mistakes that are made. Judge not; you don't know that other person's journey, but you know yours.

These mistakes can be our gold, the alchemist, as the ancient mystics said of the Philosopher's Stone, changing lead into gold. It is the act of turning our heavy thoughts, such as anger and jealousy, into feelings of forgiveness and love. Gold, as in light. Lightness of spirit. Darkness has the opposite effect. You feel heaviness in the body when feeling down and depressed, just as you feel light when you are uplifted.

Prayer: "Transform my negative beliefs into positive light, so I may live my life with more clarity and grace. Awareness radiates throughout my being as co creator with the universe and this almighty Creative Force. My inner self and I are one."

Be not afraid to admit mistakes. When we grow from our mistakes we become more confident to continue living.

With the conflicting forces that happen in life, it takes courage to live your true authentic self.

> *"It's your road, and yours alone.*
> *Others may walk it with you,*
> *but no one can walk it for you."*
>
> —*Rumi*

You are rewarded many times over, as it gives back true quality, and the value of Inner peace, which money cannot buy.

Do you know the saying, "Too much of a good thing"? Because as individuals, we have a need for pleasure, such as spending a tremendous amount of time being obsessed with video games. On the positive side, we are challenged and made aware how much encouragement we do get from each level we conquer, stimulating us to go further. On the negative side, however, it can give you nightmares.

Computer Overload Syndrome

Although you are not your body, remember your body. It loves and needs sunshine, exercise, and sport to keep fit. When you are in form, you're on top of the world. You feel good about yourself; you are sexy, inviting, open to your potential. You dance in the magic of what life has to offer.

You're in Harmony with Your Soul Journey

In this contemporary world of communication, peace and inner silence have taken a back slide. You can find ways to be in touch with your real authentic self, through forms of meditation, stilling your own mind, and listening to the silence within.

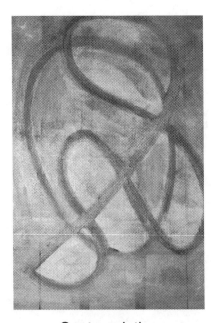

Contemplation

When you are receptive and make yourself available to this silence, you receive wonderful ideas as gifts for you to use in this complex world. We are different from artificial intelligence. Artificial intelligence will be limited, in receiving impressions from the cosmic consciousness. As humans, we are unique. We sleep, we eat, we feel, we love, we reflect. We have attitude. We are a species whom by our very nature need meaning in our lives. If we don't have meaning, we become listless and depressed and a part of our self withers away and dies.

We are inspired and moved deeply within our beings, when something touches our soul, by the smell of a rose or the sound of a child laughing. Gazing up at a deep blue sky on a warm summer's day, imagining the infinity of the cosmos. It maybe standing on the ocean shores, admiring the forever changing mood of the sea, or listening to the rhythm of the waves rolling gently to the shore.

Music, dance, drama, and the arts are creative gifts from spirit. Artists are awesome and make up a vital part of a living society.

Live creatively.

When we look at the industrial age, for example, it's like looking back at the dinosaur age. Today in the twenty-first century, humanity is experiencing an exciting time in history, as technology takes centre stage for tremendous change. However, we do not need everything surrounding us to be digital, computers and the like. It's okay for technology to make gains in the work force. It grants an opportunity for you, masters of the universe, to look at other new compelling avenues. Humans will continue to be human, and so we will continue to create stories, plays, music, fashion, and invent; to be teachers and doctors, psychologists, and farmers; along with many other jobs.

What's exciting for you, masters of the universe, is that; a great deal of these jobs have not been invented yet.

We may love social media, but we don't have to become it. We do not want our identity to become blurred with artificial intelligence; therefore, we need clearly define boundaries of who and what we are as individuals, and the future race of humans. We are dynamic beings, complex, and forever transforming into what it is we want to become. We are biological and spiritual organisms, as we interact and participate in the natural world. Cycles, beginnings, endings, and beginnings again. Although we are interconnected, our souls are unique.

Mystery of Time and Timelessness

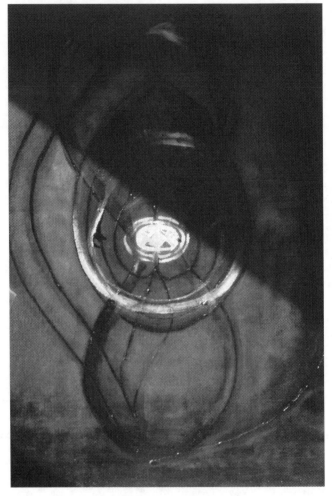

Live Your Bliss

And we dream. Don't let anyone take away your dreams. There are boundless possibilities, and it is up to you to seek them out. However, you can't just dream your dream, you have to act on it and dance through the moments of challenges that life brings. Remember, masters of the universe, happiness is not bought but is a state of mind.

It is great to have material things in the world. However, create bliss, resonate with your spirit, and understand that your spiritual self awaits your awakening. This lodestone is a powerful and natural way to discover true happiness and contentment. Experiencing the dark night of the soul is about balance; it is our challenges in life that give us mastery. It is the opening in creation to demonstrate levels where mastery of the universe is attained, an initiation to the next level.

It is an opportunity in a given moment in time, when all that we have left inside us is a speck of courage, to reach down to the deepest level of our being and test the knowledge we have gained. The earth is a school of learning for the development of souls. It is as though we accumulate all our understanding and knowledge, and then, we demand a demonstration. Okay, let's see how much we do know. Let's put it to the test.

There is a saying: "God doesn't give you what you can't handle."

Gravity, the forces at play on this earth, anchor us to the polarisation of light and dark, good and evil, and our consciousness holds the mirror up for our reflection.

Be brave, masters of the universe, when the dark night of the soul challenges you. Fear begets fear. If you want it to stay real, it will be.

However, when you heal this memory, it no longer plays a role in your life. Your authentic self grows in self-awareness, mindfulness, and playfulness.

"The secret of change is to focus all of your energy,
not on the old, but building the new."
Way of the peaceful warrior

— *Dan Millman*

Remember: Self-Awareness

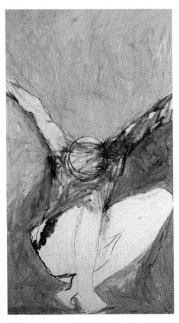

Benevolent Loving Beings Are Willing to Serve You

A couple of years back, I dreamt of an electronic flying machine; it was flying across the Gold Coast. I'm not sure if a video camera was attached, but I could see my surroundings clearly from this tiny machine. Through its eyes, I was looking at a beautifully designed mansion, built on a cliff overlooking the sea. Inside, a group of people were celebrating, having a party in their lounge room. They were not aware of this little machine or that I was watching them enjoying their afternoon, chatting among themselves. I could see the champagne glasses they were drinking from and the splendid finery which the men and women were dressed in. I didn't need the future technology dream glasses to record that dream.

To be human is to create, be innovative, to invent things. Over the course of history, we have had the capability to develop our own resources: simple things from potato peelers, hair rollers, and screw drivers to more complex things such as the computers and aeroplanes.

Our future world is going to be filled with new technology that has yet to be created. Like the thousands of drones happening right now, very similar to my dream. Drones created for agriculture, drones to carry cameras for filmmakers, ambulance drones, drones for surveying sharks over ocean shorelines, even drones for humans to fly in. Ehang Inc. has successfully designed a one man flying drone which has four doubled propellers that spin parallel to the ground.

In addition, bionic limbs and robotic devices to assist walking, there are touchscreen furniture that we can play interactive games on, multi-display computer setups for every day, and even computer wrist bands. Wifi soon will be obsolete as LiFi takes over, so we can connect to the internet in our own homes from light bulbs.

As Gabriel Craven from ITG Technology says, "Back in the 'old' days, in the fifties, sixties, and seventies, people had to go out of their houses to socialise, to do things, to meet people.

"And … a conversation was a conversation with that person.

"Now, they still go out, but look anywhere, in restaurants, on a bus or train, even walking down the street, people are on their phones, communicating.

"Don't have a fear of robots; have a fear of turning humans into robots."

This is just the beginning.

Awake to Your Consciousness and Surroundings

Remember the power of a loving heart.
Thank you, my sisters and brothers; you have done well.
Be strong in your mastery of the universe and self.
Your youth is vital for the growth of the twenty-first century.
To live in harmony with artificial intelligence is a requisite.

We are not machines; we dream in many ways.

"The future belongs to those who believe
in the beauty of their dreams."
— Eleanor Roosevelt

This is your calling, youth of the twenty-first century, masters of the universe.

I invite you to travel the realms of the universe. Who knows? I may see you there.

Serving the Greater Light

I am that I am

There is no separation.

You Are Home

Printed in the United States
By Bookmasters